Summer Fun

by Jennifer Waters

Content and Reading Adviser: Joan Stewart
Educational Consultant/Literacy Specialist
New York Public Schools

Spyglass BOOKS

COMPASS POINT BOOKS

Minneapolis, Minnesota

Compass Point Books
3722 West 50th Street, #115
Minneapolis, MN 55410

Visit Compass Point Books on the Internet at *www.compasspointbooks.com*
or e-mail your request to *custserv@compasspointbooks.com*

Photographs ©:
DigitalVision, cover; Comstock, 5, 7, 9; Visuals Unlimited/Mark E. Gibson, 11; Corel, 13;
Comstock, 15; Two Coyote Studios/Mary Walker Foley, 17; Comstock, 19; Two Coyote
Studios/Mary Walker Foley, 20, 21.

Project Manager: Rebecca Weber McEwen
Editor: Alison Auch
Photo Researcher: Jennifer Waters
Photo Selectors: Rebecca Weber McEwen and Jennifer Waters
Design: Mary Walker Foley

Library of Congress Cataloging-in-Publication Data

Waters, Jennifer.
  Summer fun / by Jennifer Waters.
    p. cm. -- (Spyglass books)
Includes bibliographical references and index.
  ISBN 0-7565-0244-6 (hardcover)
  1. Summer--Juvenile literature. [1. Summer. 2. Play.] I. Title. II.
Series.
  QB637.6 .W37 2002
  508.2--dc21
                              2001007327

Contents

Summer

Summer days can be long and hot, but they are filled with fun in the sun.

Summer happens when the north half of Earth is tilted toward the sun.

North half of Earth

Sun →

Playing in
a sprinkler

Nice, Cool Pools

Playing in water is
a good way to cool off
on a hot summer day.

Outdoor swimming pools
are open for the season.
It's the perfect time to go
for a swim.

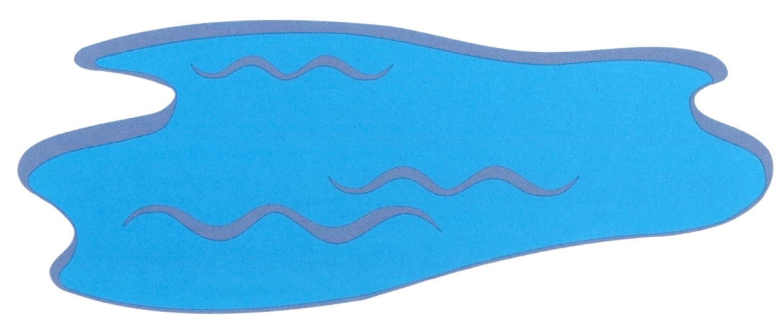

Goggles
protect
your eyes
under
the water.

7

Snow Cones and Ice Cream

Snow-cone stands and ice-cream shops are busy when the weather is hot.

Sometimes ice-cream trucks drive around. The driver stops when people want to buy some cold ice cream.

Fairs and Festivals

Summer is the time for *fairs* and summer *festivals*.
Fairs and festivals are held outdoors in the warm weather.

People like to eat food and play games at fairs and festivals. Many fairs have *carnival* rides and live music.

People enjoy exciting rides in the summer.

Water Parks and Amusement Parks

Some people can hardly wait for water parks and *amusement* parks to open for the summer.

Playing in the water or going on wild rides is great summer fun.

Tunnels in
a water slide
are cool, wet,
and slippery!

13

Summer Camping

Going to summer camp can be exciting. Kids can go to adventure camps, acting camps, and even magic camps!

Some families go to the mountains or the countryside to camp in the summer.

Tents can help
people stay warm
and dry when
they are camping.

15

Fireworks Shows

The best fireworks shows happen during the summer. The biggest fireworks shows happen on July 4, which is America's **Independence Day**.

Sometimes there are fireworks at baseball games, fairs, and festivals.

Fireworks light up
the dark night sky.

The Beach

For many people, summertime means beach time. Spending the day at the ocean or at a lake is great summer fun.

When they are at the beach, people wear sunscreen as protection from the sun's rays.

These girls are building a sand castle.

19

Summer Rain Painting

What you'll need:

- A rainy day
- White crayon
- Food coloring
- Paper plates (uncoated)

1. Draw a design on the plate with the crayon.

2. Sprinkle drops of food coloring onto the design.

3. Put on rain gear, and take your plate outside.

4. Let the rain fall onto the plate.

5. Tilt the plate in different directions to make colorful designs.

Glossary

amusement—something that is fun and entertaining

carnival—a traveling show that has rides and games

fair—a place where people bring animals or food they have raised and compete for prizes. Fairs also have fun things for visitors to do.

festival—where people gather to listen to music and look at art

Independence Day—the celebration of the day the people of the United States decided to form their own country

Learn More

Books

Maslen, Bobby Lynn. *Summer*. New York: Scholastic, 1996.

Saunders-Smith, Gail. *Summer*. Mankato, Minn.: Pebble Books, 1998.

Schweninger, Ann. *Summertime*. New York: Viking Penguin, 1992.

Web Site

Brain Pop

www.brainpop.com/science/seeall.weml
(click on "seasons")

www.brainpop.com/tech/seeall.weml
(click on "fireworks")

Index

GR: F

Word Count: 261

From Jennifer Waters

I live near the Rocky Mountains.
The ocean is my favorite place.
I like to write songs and books.
I hope you enjoyed this book.

24